OUTLAWS AND SHERIFFS

Vic Kovacs

PowerKiDS
press

Published in 2016 by **The Rosen Publishing Group, Inc.**
29 East 21st Street, New York, NY 10010

Developed and produced for Rosen by BlueAppleWorks Inc.

Art Director: T.J. Choleva
Managing Editor for BlueAppleWorks: Melissa McClellan
Designer: Joshua Avramson
Photo Research: Jane Reid
Editor: Rachel Stuckey

Illustration & Photo Credits: Cover, p, 5, 6-7, 23 Frederic Remington/ Public Domain; title page Alfred Jacob Miller/Public Domain; cover, title page, back cover (skull) Jim Parkin/Shutterstock; cover, title page (wood) Dagmara_K/Shutterstock; back cover background homydesign/ Shutterstock; background siro46/Shutterstock; chapter intro backgrounds rangizzz/Shutterstock; p. 8, 12, 15, 20, 24, 25, 26 Carlyn Iverson; p. 18 Comstock/Thinkstock; p. 28 Charles Marion Russell/Public Domain

Cataloging-in-Publication-Data

Kovacs, Vic.
Outlaws and sheriffs / by Vic Kovacs.
p. cm. — (The true history of the Wild West)
Includes index.
ISBN 978-1-4994-1178-2 (pbk.)
ISBN 978-1-4994-1206-2 (6-pack)
ISBN 978-1-4994-1197-3 (library binding)
1. Outlaws — West (U.S.) — Biography — Juvenile literature.
2. Peace officers — West (U.S.) — Biography — Juvenile literature.
3. Frontier and pioneer life — West (U.S.) — Juvenile literature.
I. Title.
F594.K68 2016
978'.02'0922—d23

Manufactured in the United States of America

CPSIA Compliance Information: Batch #WS15PK
For Further Information contact: Rosen Publishing, New York, New York at 1-800-237-9932

CONTENTS

Outlaws and sheriffs often clashed in the
wilderness surrounding the Wild West towns.

Wild West Foes

The Wild West was home to all kinds of people. Farmers, ranchers, cowboys, Native Americans, and recent immigrants made the West a unique part of American history. Two types of people that stand out in the Wild West were outlaws and sheriffs. They were usually on opposite sides of the law, but often had more in common than you might think. A feared gunfighter in one territory might be a respected lawman in another. As America spread westward it was difficult to enforce the law in the new territories. Lawlessness was common, especially on the open trail and in rural areas where there were few people. It took time to set up town governments and legal systems. Many people took advantage of this to take what they wanted and live how they chose.

Outlaws usually worked in gangs because there is safety in numbers.

Outlaws

In the early days of the Wild West, it took time for the law to catch up with new settlements and towns. Some people took the opportunity to make their fortunes through dishonest means. Many were bandits, and most worked with some kind of gang. Some people became bandits or **rustlers** who worked together in gangs. The myth of the Wild West includes stories of bank robberies, but these were very rare. Rustlers made money by stealing horses and cattle and reselling them. And bandits robbed stagecoaches and wagon trains on the open frontier. In later years, outlaws would rob trains as they traveled through unoccupied territory.

Sheriffs

Lawmen in the Wild West had many titles. There were the marshals, who worked for the federal government. There were also state lawmen, like the Texas Rangers. Some towns, like Abilene, Texas, had local police forces. But the most well-known lawman in the west was the sheriff. The county sheriff was in charge of enforcing the law in any town within the borders of the county. Sheriffs were usually elected and then free to appoint their deputies, officers who enforced the law under the sheriff's authority. If there wasn't enough money to hire full-time deputies, in a crisis the sheriff also had the power to recruit able-bodied men to form a **posse**.

Jesse and his older brother Frank James are famous Wild West outlaws. They led the James–Younger Gang after the Civil War.

Jesse James

Jesse James was one of the most famous outlaws of the Wild West. Hailing from Missouri, Jesse joined a group of **Confederate guerrilla fighters** when he was fifteen. Jesse's unit once massacred over twenty unarmed **Union** soldiers. Even after the war ended, there was still a lot of conflict between the two sides in Missouri. Jesse and his older brother Frank joined in anti-Union attacks. The first daytime bank robbery in the U.S. was part of this conflict. Legend has it that the James brothers were there in 1866, but there is no proof.

The first known robbery committed by the James brothers was on December 7th, 1869. During the robbery they killed a cashier, who they mistakenly thought was the man who had killed Jesse's wartime **mentor**. They didn't get much money, but they managed to escape the posse sent to catch them.

The robbery and murder were reported in the newspaper, and Jesse liked the attention. The James brothers teamed up with Jim and Bob Younger, and some other men, to form the James-Younger gang.

Many Confederates were still upset about losing the Civil War, and Jesse used this to his advantage. He often sent letters to newspapers to claim that he only robbed pro-Union Republicans. Soon the public saw James as a kind of Robin Hood, who only stole from the rich and powerful. Of course, the James-Younger Gang kept their loot, instead of giving it to the poor.

After a failed robbery that left most of his gang killed or captured, Jesse retired for a few years. But he soon grew restless and recruited a new gang in 1879. Unlike the old gang of former Confederate guerrillas, the new gang was made up of common thieves.

In 1881, Missouri governor Thomas T. Crittenden offered a $10,000 cash reward for the gang members' capture, dead or alive. By 1882, the only members left were a pair of brothers, Charley and Robert Ford.

MYTH: The Wild West was a violent place.

TRUTH OR MYTH? This is a myth. The Wild West was actually safer than most modern American cities. In fact, the entire American west had about the same murder rate as East St. Louis, Illinois, does today. Even cities with the bloodiest reputations had shockingly few incidents of violence. Take the **notorious** Deadwood, South Dakota. The most murders it saw in a single year was four. At the height of the **cattle drive** era, busy towns along the trail were full of cowboys and gamblers. But from 1879 to 1885, the five busiest towns from Abilene to Wichita had only 45 murders combined. The reality is, you were much more likely to die from an untreatable illness in the Wild West than you were from violence.

When Robert heard about the reward, he met with the governor of Missouri about bringing Jesse in. On April 3rd, 1882, just before leaving with the Ford brothers to pull another robbery, Jesse noticed a picture on his wall was crooked. As Jesse turned to adjust the frame, Robert shot him in the back of the head.

11

Train robbers often rode the train as passengers before their gang stopped the train to rob it.

Train Robbers

Most train robberies in the Wild West happened between 1865 and 1875. It was far too difficult to rob banks in town, and much easier to stop a train in the middle of nowhere. Eventually, the railways increased security and train robberies became too risky.

The target of train robberies were usually payroll shipments kept in safes on special "express cars." The robbers would force the guards to give up the combination. If that didn't work, robbers would use **dynamite** to blow up the safe, or take the safe with them. The gang would often turn on the passengers too. Given the choice of keeping their valuables or their lives, most passengers handed over their cash or jewelry. With their loot secured, the bandits would ride off, often leaving the train, and everyone on it, stranded.

MYTH: Train robbers leapt on to moving trains from horseback.

TRUTH OR MYTH? This is a myth. While trains were slower than they are today, thieves couldn't jump onto moving trains from horseback like in the movies. If they did they'd be riding away with broken bones instead of loot. Instead, there were two main methods of robbing trains. In the first and safest method, the bandits would board the train like regular passengers. Then, once the journey was underway, they would reveal themselves and begin the holdup. The other more dangerous method involved forcing the train to stop, usually in an area far away from any towns or settlements.

The Reno Brothers

The first peacetime train robbery in American history happened the night of October 6th, 1866. The Reno gang included four brothers, Frank, John, Sim, and Bill Reno, and a few other outlaws. On that night, members of the Reno gang boarded a train at the station in Seymour, Indiana. At first they seemed like regular passengers. Once the train was a safe distance from town, they put on masks and headed to the express car. At gunpoint, the guard opened the smaller safe but claimed he couldn't open the larger safe. So the robbers pushed the safe off of the train and leapt after it. The Reno gang never got the large safe open, but they still managed to escape with about $12,000.

This single robbery was the beginning of on era. Train robberies soon became an iconic part of the Wild West.

Butch Cassidy's Wild Bunch

The robber known as Butch Cassidy robbed his first bank in 1889, when he was twenty-three. In 1896, he formed a notorious outlaw gang called the Wild Bunch. Cassidy encouraged this group to avoid violence as much as possible, and Cassidy himself claimed to have never killed a man.The Wild Bunch's specialty was robbing trains.

In one spectacular job, near Wilcox, Wyoming, they used so much dynamite to open the mail and express cars, and the safe inside, that there was almost no train left! It was the success of the Wild Bunch and other gangs that made railways improve their security. This made it harder to pull off a job. In 1901, Butch Cassidy, along with his friend known as the Sundance Kid, fled to South America to continue to enjoy the outlaw lifestyle. It's believed they were killed in Bolivia, but there were rumors that they returned home and lived quietly.

The Union Pacific Big Springs Robbery

Sam Bass came to Nebraska on a cattle drive with his friend Joel Collins in 1875. After selling the herd, they didn't take the money back to the Texas ranchers who hired them. Instead they spent all $8,000, and then turned to robbery to support themselves. Disappointed with robbing stagecoaches, Bass decided that trains would be more worth their while. Bass and Collins learned that a train belonging to the Union Pacific Railroad would be passing through Big Springs on the evening of

The Gentleman Bandit

Many bandits were rough men, but not all of them. Take Bill Miner, who was also known as "The Gentleman Bandit." A snappy dresser with a silver tongue, Miner was a well-known robber of stagecoaches and trains. Why was he so well known? His manners! Miner was said to be always polite to his victims, even when he was parting them from their most valued possessions. He sometimes even apologized. He's also credited with coining the phrase "Hands up," making him one of the most influential criminals of all time.

September 18th, 1875. That night, they forced the depot agent in charge to signal for the train to stop. On board, they found out that the safe was on a timer, and couldn't be opened. About to leave nearly empty-handed, they noticed some wooden boxes. Inside one box, they found brand new $20 gold pieces! After raiding all the boxes, they had about $60,000 worth of gold. For good measure, they robbed all of the train's passengers on their way out. This is still the largest robbery of a Union Pacific train in history.

Unlike in Hollywood movies, gun fights were uncommon in the real Wild West.

Quick Guns

While gunfights did happen in the Wild West, they were not the way we imagine them. Two lone men outdrawing each other on a dusty street, testing their marksmanship and speed, was a rare sight. Gunfights happened on the spur of the moment. Fighters ducked for cover firing as many shots as they could. Shootouts often began as disputes in the saloon and alcohol affected the fighters' aim. Bystanders were often hit. Guns were emptied, and the gun smoke could be so thick that it would take minutes to see if anyone had actually "won." People known for their skills with a gun came from different paths. Some were bandits, some were cowboys, some were gamblers. But whatever their reason for taking up the gun, if they weren't lawmen, they were outlaws.

Billy the Kid

William Henry McCarty, alias William H. Bonney, alias Billy the Kid, was a petty thief by the time he was fourteen. After escaping from a jail in Silver City, New Mexico, he got his start stealing horses. In 1877, he killed his first man. Windy Cahill was a bully who enjoyed tormenting Billy, who was small and skinny. Either in retaliation or in self defense, Billy shot Cahill in the gut on August 17th, and fled. Billy was about seventeen at the time of this shooting.

The Kid ended up in Lincoln County, New Mexico, where he worked as a ranch hand for a local businessman named John Tunstall. During a rancher conflict called the Lincoln County War, Tunstall was killed. Billy and the other ranch hands formed a group called the Regulators to get justice. After a series of gunfights that left many on both sides dead, Billy fled and started his own gang. He lived as a fugitive until he was caught and killed by Sheriff Pat Garrett in 1881.

MYTH: Famous gunmen shot scores of people all the time.

TRUTH OR MYTH? This is a myth. Gunfighters on both sides of the law did shoot people. However, the exact numbers were greatly exaggerated both by the gunfighters themselves and by newspapers. The gunfighters hoped to establish a fearsome reputation. Newspapers did it to sell more copies. Publishers thought that the more fantastic a story was, the more people would want to read it. A popular legend claims Billy the Kid killed twenty-one men, one for every year of his life. The number that have been proven is closer to seven.

John Wesley Hardin

John Wesley Hardin was born in Texas in 1853. He spread death wherever he went, killing men in self-defense, to avoid paying bills, and even as bets. He was said to have a temper that was almost as quick as his draw. It's not known how many men he killed before he was arrested and sentenced to 25 years in prison in 1878. Hardin claimed he had over forty victims, but experts today place the number at around half of that.

Sheriffs in the Wild West had to be tough, strong men and very good riders.

Tough Sheriffs

Being a lawman in the Wild West could be a thankless, dangerous job. Many were former outlaws who switched sides for stability and the promise of a regular paycheck. Others honestly wished to bring a bit of order to the lawless frontier. Skill with a gun was a necessity, and often meant the difference between life and death. A number of gifted gunfighters became sheriffs, and would use their fearsome reputations to discourage crime. After all, if you knew breaking the law meant facing down one of the quickest guns in the west, you'd probably think twice!

Wyatt Earp

The third of five brothers, Wyatt Earp was born in Illinois in 1848. As an adult, he roamed the frontier, working a number of different jobs. But he always ended up returning to what made him an icon: law enforcement.

Earp worked as a police officer in Wichita, Kansas, and an assistant marshal in Dodge City, in the same state. But it was in Tombstone, Arizona, where Wyatt became a legend. The Gunfight at the O.K. Corral is the most famous gun battle in the history of the Wild West. Local cowboy outlaws had a grudge against Wyatt's brother Virgil, who was the town marshal. Then a deputy marshal, Wyatt Earp, his friend Doc Holliday, and his brother Morgan who was also a marshal, came to Virgil's aid. On October 26th, 1881, the feud exploded on the streets of Tombstone, near the horse stables. The famous fight lasted only about 30 seconds. When it was over, three of the outlaws were killed. In the months following the fight, Virgil was wounded and Morgan was killed as payback by the remaining outlaws. Looking for revenge, Wyatt rounded up a **vigilante** posse and tracked and killed the men he held responsible. Rather than face trial, Wyatt left the state. He eventually settled in California, where he lived peacefully for the rest of his life.

Pat Garrett

Pat Garrett is best known as the lawman who finally killed Billy the Kid. But before becoming Sheriff, Garrett had worked as a cowboy, a buffalo hunter, and a saloon keeper. He was also a friend of Billy the Kid. In 1880, after the Lincoln County War, Garrett was given the job of county sheriff. He swore to track down Billy the Kid, who was on the run and rustling livestock. Garrett kept his promise, and caught the Kid on December 23rd, 1880. Billy the Kid was sentenced to death, but manged to escape his jail cell in April of 1881, killing two guards in the process. Garrett tracked the Kid to his friend Peter Maxwell's ranch. According to Garrett, he was talking to Maxwell in a dark room when Billy came in. Unable to see who was in the room, Billy asked "Who's there?" in Spanish. Without saying a word, Garrett shot Billy the Kid twice, killing him.

Wild Bill Hickok

Wild Bill Hickok learned to shoot a gun while he was still a boy, and quickly became a crack shot. He also knew the value of a reputation, and was happy to let the press exaggerate stories about him. One example is the McCanles Massacre. While Hickok was working at a **Pony Express** station, a man named David McCanles came in with two friends to collect a debt. An argument broke out and gunfire was exchanged. McCanles was shot dead and his friends would later die of their injuries. Every time the story was reported in the newspapers, the number of men killed would get higher and higher. Hickok claimed to have killed as many as 100 men, and that he fought and killed a bear with nothing but a knife.

This reputation would come in handy when Hickok worked as a lawman in dangerous frontier towns like Abilene.

When people think of the Wild West, guns are one of the first things that come to mind. This image is true of people making their way along trails, driving cattle, and living on the frontier. But carrying guns inside town limits was often illegal. Upon entering town, gun owners dropped their guns off at the sheriff's office. They would get a token or ticket in return. It was very similar to the modern-day coat check. In many of the most "violent" towns in the west, like Tombstone and Dodge City, carrying guns was against the law. In fact, the first law Dodge City passed was to forbid the carrying of **concealed** weapons. History shows that the second leading reason for arrest in frontier towns was illegally carrying a gun.

However, after accidentally killing one of his deputies during a gunfight, he was fired and started working as a gambler. In 1876 in Deadwood, during a game of poker, Hickok was shot in the back of the head by a man named Jack McCall—for reasons that are still unknown today. Hickok's poker hand at the time, two eights and two aces, is now known as the Dead Man's Hand.

Law in Force

By the end of the 19th century, lawlessness was on the decline. As more and more people moved westward and more and more towns sprung up, the wide open spaces of the frontier began to disappear. With fewer places to hide, and increasingly strict laws all over the country, living outside the law stopped being as profitable as it once was. With increased security on trains, and Sheriff's departments growing along with their towns and counties, robberies and holdups were no longer sources of easy money.

As the 20th century arrived, enforcing law and order was easier. The Wild West era of outlaw gangs and public shootouts was over.

When gold was found in California in 1848, people streamed in from all over, hoping to make their fortunes. This huge **influx** of people **overwhelmed** the established organizations in charge of enforcing the law. In the face of widespread lawlessness, in 1852, at the height of the gold rush, the Los Angeles Rangers was founded. Originally a state militia, the Rangers would later grow into both the Los Angeles Police Department and the Los Angeles County Sheriff's Department, which today is the largest sheriff's department in the country. At the time, they helped the new state to enforce some much needed law and order.

Today, there are still people who operate outside the law, but attitudes have changed. The job of sheriff changed as well. Many local police forces grew out of local sheriff's departments. There are still sheriffs in the United States, but their jobs vary across the country. In many cases, they are the highest law enforcement official in a county. Sheriffs often police areas in their county that aren't within city or town limits and enforce court orders and warrants. With over 3,000 sheriff's offices in the U.S., they run the full range of law enforcement.

Glossary

cattle drive The moving of large herds of cattle from the ranches to towns where they were sold.

concealed Hidden from view.

Confederate From the southern states that separated from the United States and fought against the Union in the Civil War.

dynamite A powerful and dangerous explosive.

guerrilla fighters Small groups of militia or independent fighters who use nontraditional methods to fight a war.

influx An arrival or entry of large numbers of people or things.

mentor An experienced and trusted adviser.

notorious Famous or well-known, usually for a bad reason.

overwhelmed Caused (someone) to have too many things to deal with.

Pony Express A mail service that used horse riders to deliver the mail from St. Louis to California in the early 1860s.

posse A group of armed men organized by a lawman to help enforce the law.

rustler A person who steals livestock like horses or cattle using cowboy skills.

Union The northern states that did not secede from the United States and which fought against the Confederacy in the Civil War.

vigilante A person who punishes criminals outside the legal process, such as by killing a killer.

For More Information

Further Reading

Hicks, Peter. *You Wouldn't Want to Live in a Wild West Town!* New York, NY: Scholastic, Revised edition, 2013.

Nelson, Vaunda Micheaux. *Bad News for Outlaws: The Remarkable Life of Bass Reeves, Deputy U.S. Marshal.* Minneapolis, MN: Carolrhoda Books, 2013.

Woog, Adam. *Jesse James: The Wild West for Kids.* New York, NY: Sky Pony Press, 2014.

Woog, Adam. *Wyatt Earp.* New York, NY: Chelsea House Pub, 2010.

Websites

Due to the changing nature of Internet links, PowerKids Press has developed an online list of websites related to the subject of this book. This site is updated regularly. Please use this link to access the list:
www.powerkidslinks.com/thoww/outlaws

Index